WHAT IF...?

Sheila Pitts
What If...?

Published by BooxAI

ISBN: 978-965-578-157-1

WHAT IF...?

SHEILA PITTS

CONTENTS

I would like to dedicate this book to my family and friends who have encouraged me to use my GOD given gift to write poems.

want to thank my Pastor, Bishop Charles JJ Jackson III and Co-Pastor, Alaine ackson of Cornerstone Baptist Church in Spartanburg, SC for their leadership and teaching. I also would like to thank Pastor Bessie Black of Westminster Presbyterian Church of Saxon, SC for her leadership and teaching.

INTRODUCTION

WHAT IF...? WITHOUT A DOUBT

GIVES YOU SOMETHING TO THINK ABOUT

PERHAPS YOU NEVER CONSIDERED BEFORE

SO WHAT IF I IMPLORE

WHAT IF...? CAUSES YOU TO MEDITATE

AS YOU CONTEMPLATE THEN ACTIVATE

SO TODAY YOU CAN CHOOSE

RIGHT OR WRONG, WIN OR LOSE

WHAT IF CHRIST CAME BACK FOR ME

WHERE WOULD MY DESTINATION BE

WHERE WOULD I SPEND ETERNITY

HEAVEN OR HELL UNDENIABLY

WHAT IF I NEVER BELIEVED IN JESUS CHRIST

AND THAT HE WAS THE ULTIMATE SACRIFICE?

(JOHN 3:16; HEBREWS 10:11-12; 1 CORINTHIANS 5:7 B)

WHAT IF I NEGLECTED TO PRAY

AND CHRISTIAN LOVE I DID NOT DISPLAY?

THESSALONIANS 5:17; JOHN 15:12, 17; JAMES 2:8; I PETER 2:17B)

WHAT IF I ALLOWED OTHERS TO PRAISE ME

INSTEAD OF GIVING GOD HIS GLORY?

(ISAIAH 43:7; ISAIAH 42:8)

WHAT IF I ALLOW THE LOVE OF MONEY

TO LEAD ME INTO IDOLATRY?

TIMOTHY 6:10)

WHAT IF I BELITTLE OR DESPISE MY NEIGHBOR

INSTEAD OF ENCOURAGING EACH ANOTHER?

(PROVERBS 11:12; 1 THESSALONIANS 5:11, 14; JAMES 2:8)

WHAT IF I SHOWED PARTIALITY

ENVY, RIVALRY AND JEALOUSY?

TIMOTHY 5:21; GALATIANS 5:20, 21, 26)

WHAT IF I TOOK MONEY

OR ANYTHING THAT DID NOT BELONG TO ME?

(EXODUS 20:15; EPHESIANS 4:28)

WHAT IF I WAS ALWAYS JUDGING

INSTEAD OF PRAYING AND INTERCEDING?

(MATTHEW 7:1-2; JAMES 5:16)

WHAT IF I DID NOT STRIVE TO LIVE IN PEACE

AND WICKEDNESS I WOULD NOT CEASE?

(HEBREW 12:14; PROVERBS 10:27-30; 15:9,26,28,29; 17:13,15; ISAIAH 59:2)

WHAT IF I CONTINUED TO DO

WHATEVER I WANTED TO?

PROVERBS 16:25; GALATIANS 6:7-8)

WHAT IF I WANTED TO BE

IN CHARGE OF MY DESTINY?

(ROMANS 6:16-23)

WHAT IF I WAS NOT SO INNOCENT

AND THE RIGHTEOUS I RESENT?

(JAMES 2:10; PSALM 34:21B-22)

WHAT IF CHRIST I DENIED

WHILE THE FLESH I GRATIFIED?

(2 TIMOTHY 2:12; GALATIANS 5:19-21)

WHAT IF I SAY FOR CHRIST I LIVE

BUT MY SISTER OR BROTHER I DID NOT FORGIVE?

(ROMANS 14:8; MATTHEW 6:15)

WHAT IF I WAS WISE

BUT ONLY IN MY OWN EYES?

(PROVERBS 3:7-8; PROVERBS 26:12)

WHAT IF I TRIED TO HURT GOD'S MESSENGER

WITH FALSE ACCUSATIONS AND SLANDER?

CHRONICLES 16:22; PSALM 105:15)

WHAT IF I CONTINUALLY TOLD LIES

AND TRIED TO COVER WITH FALSE ALIBIS?

(PROVERBS 12:22; PROVERBS 13:5; COLOSSIANS 3:9-10)

WHAT IF I CAUSED STRIFE

WITH OTHERS IN MY LIFE?

(PROVERBS 16:28; PROVERBS 17:14; 29:22)

WHAT IF I HAD A PROUD SPIRIT

AND THOUGHT THAT I WAS THE IT.

(PROVERBS 16:5, 18-19; PROVERBS 6:16-17; 29:23)

WHAT IF I HAD A WICKED HEART

AND TROUBLE I WOULD ALWAYS START?

(PROVERBS 11:5B, 23B; PROVERBS 6:14-19)

WHAT IF I LOOKED FOR WAYS TO

CAUSE CHAOS AND DIDN'T CARE WHO KNEW?

(PROVERBS 6:16-19; 28:5A, 13A, 18B)

WHAT IF I SEEKED TO HURT OTHERS

EVEN MY SISTERS AND BROTHERS?

(PROVERBS 6:16-19)

WHAT IF I LACKED COMPASSION

AND PLEASING ME WAS MY PASSION?

(MATTHEW 25:31-46; I JOHN 3:17-18)

WHAT IF I WAS DISOBEDIENT

AND REFUSED TO REPENT?

(PSALM 1:5, 6; TITUS 1:16; LUKE 13:3, 5; ACTS 26:13-20)

WHAT IF I CAUSED SOMEONE TO REJECT

THE CHRIST WHOM I FAILED TO REFLECT?

(1 PETER 2:12)

WHAT IF DOING THINGS MY WAY

CAUSED OTHERS TO GO ASTRAY?

(PROVERBS 14:25,34-35; 18:21; 20:7)

WHAT IF THE RIGHTEOUS I DESPISE

AS I CAUSE STRIFE AND UTTER LIES?

(PSALM 34:21; PROVERBS 11:8-9,27; 12:2,13,17-18,27,30-31)

WHAT IF I CAUSED OTHERS TO DENY

THE CHRIST I FAIL TO EXEMPLIFY?

PETER 2:12)

WHAT IF MY LIGHT FAILED TO SHINE

BECAUSE IT WAS NOT GENUINE?

(1 JOHN 2:8-11)

WHAT IF I WAS HEARD

TALKING AND BEING ABSURD?

(TITUS 2:7-8)

WHAT IF I CAUSED SHEEP TO SCATTER

BECAUSE I DIDN'T THINK THEY MATTER?

(JEREMIAH 23:1-4)

O YOU THINK GOD WOULD BE PLEASED

F I DID ANY OF THESE?

THESSALONIANS 4:1-18)

WHAT IF TODAY...?

WHAT IF STARTING TODAY

I DID THINGS GOD'S WAY?

WHAT IF I REPENT TODAY

AND QUIT DOING THINGS MY WAY?

WHAT IF I STOP TODAY

TO KNEEL AND PRAY?

WHAT IF TODAY

I REFUSE TO GO ASTRAY?

WHAT IF TODAY

I REFUSE TO LET MY PRIDE GET IN THE WAY?

WHAT IF TODAY

I LISTEN AND OBEY?

WHAT IF TODAY

N SIN I REFUSE TO STAY?

WHAT IF TODAY

I MONITOR THE WORDS I SAY?

WHAT IF TODAY

I COMMIT TO GOD'S WAY?

WHAT IF TODAY

REFUSE TO LET FEAR GET IN THE WAY?

WHAT IF TRUTH...?

WHAT IF THE TRUTH I CONCEALED

AND NEVER REVEALED?

WHAT IF WHAT I KNEW

COULD HELP OTHERS TOO?

WHAT IF I CAUSED OTHERS TO FAIL

BECAUSE THE TRUTH I DID NOT TELL?

WHAT IF BY TELLING THE TRUTH

IMPACT THE FUTURE OF OUR YOUTH?

WHAT IF CHRIST I DENY

BY TEACHING A LIE?

WHAT IF FEAR...?

WHAT IF FEAR CAUSED ME

DEFEAT INSTEAD OF VICTORY?

WHAT IF FEAR CAUSED ME

TO SURRENDER TO THE ENEMY?

WHAT IF BECAUSE OF FEAR

I DIDN'T ADVANCE I'M STILL HERE?

WHAT IF FEAR CAUSED ME TO FAIL

BECAUSE I GAVE UP AND DID NOT PREVAIL?

WHAT IF FEAR CAUSED ME

TO BE BOUND AND NOT SET FREE?

WHAT IF FEAR CAUSED ME

TO BE BLIND AND NOT SEE?

WHAT IF FEAR PREVENTED ME

FROM BEING BLESSED SPIRITUALLY?

WHAT IF FEAR PREVENTED ME

FROM REACHING MY DESTINY?

WHAT IF FEAR CAUSED ME TO GO ASTRAY

AND LOSE FOCUS ALONG THE WAY?

WHAT IF BECAUSE OF FEAR

DOUBT AND UNBELIEF APPEAR?

WHAT IF BECAUSE I WAS AFRAID

IN AN ABUSIVE RELATIONSHIP I STAYED?

WHAT IF...?
PART 2

HAT IF I DIDN'T TRY

JT ONLY DID ENOUGH TO GET BY?

HAT IF MY PERSONALITY

EVEALED MY IMMATURITY?

WHAT IF I HAD THE ABILITY

BUT FAILED BECAUSE I WAS LAZY?

WHAT IF FOLLOWING A PERSON

LED ME IN THE WRONG DIRECTION?

WHAT IF HUMILITY

WILL ALLOW GOD TO USE ME?

WHAT IF I QUIT MAKING AN EXCUSE

AND BECOME THE VESSEL THAT GOD CAN USE?

WHAT IF I LET GO OF THE PAST

AND THE THINGS THAT WON'T LAST?

WHAT IF I THINK ON THINGS AS ETERNAL

AND NOT ON THINGS THAT ARE CARNAL?

WHAT IF I DON'T ABUSE THE AUTHORITY

THAT GOD HAS GIVEN ME?

WHAT IF I FAILED TO

THINK THINGS THROUGH?

WHAT IF I WAS ALWAYS NEGATIVE

AND NEVER POSITIVE?

WHAT IF...?
PART 3

HAT IF I DIDN'T GET MY REST

HE NIGHT BEFORE I TOOK THE TEST?

HAT IF I REFUSED TO

JRN IN HOMEWORK WHEN DUE?

WHAT IF I WOULD SWEAR

BUT DIDN'T SEE MY TEACHER SITTING THERE?

WHAT IF I HAD TOO MANY TARDIES

WITH NO WRITTEN EXCUSES?

WHAT IF I DIDN'T PAY ATTENTION

AND FOLLOW DIRECTION?

HAT IF I FAILED TO GIVE MY PARENT

HE NOTE MY TEACHER SENT?

HAT IF I MADE A C

HEN I COULD HAVE MADE A B?

HAT IF I PLAYED HOOKY

ND RAN INTO MY MOMMY (DADDY)?

WHAT IF, A LACK OF PREPARATION

CAUSED FRUSTRATION?

WHAT IF I ACTED LIKE A FOOL

AND HAD DETENTION AFTER SCHOOL?

WHAT IF I FAILED TO STUDY

AND MADE A D.

WHAT IF I NEVER BELIEVED

I NEVER RECEIVED
SALVATION
BUT CONDEMNATION
BECAUSE I NEVER HEARD
ABOUT THE WORD
IF SALVATION IS FREE
WHY NO ONE TOLD ME

**SO TODAY I AM TELLING YOU
ABOUT THE ONLY ONE WHO
WAS CRUCIFIED ON THE CROSS
SO THAT YOU WOULD NOT BE LOST**

OR GOD SO LOVETH THE WORLD THAT HE GAVE HIS ONLY EGOTTEN SON, THAT WHOSOEVER BELIEVETH IN HIM HOULD NOT PERISH, BUT HAVE EVERLASTING LIFE." (JOHN 6)

HAT IF THOU SHALT CONFESS WITH THY MOUTH THE LORD SUS, AND SHALT BELIEVE IN THINE HEART THAT GOD HATH AISED HIM FROM THE DEAD, THOU SHALT BE SAVED." OM.10:9)

OR WITH THE HEART MAN BELIEVETH UNTO RIGHT-OUSNESS; AND WITH THE MOUTH CONFESSION IS MADE NTO SALVATION." (ROMANS 10:10)

GOD COVERED ME

**AS I WENT
TO REPENT
SEEKING FORGIVENESS
OF MY MESS**

FROM A REPENTANT HEART
I GOT A FRESH START
ON ME GOD POURED
HIS LOVE AND RESTORED
I WAS NOT EXPOSED
BECAUSE HE CHOSE
TO COVER ME
SO I COULD BE

JUSTIFIED

AND SANCTIFIED

TO FULFILL

HIS DIVINE WILL

ESUS SAITH UNTO HIM, I AM THE WAY, THE TRUTH, AND THE FE: NO MAN COMETH UNTO THE FATHER, BUT BY ME."JOHN 4:6

THERE IS A WAY WHICH SEEMETH RIGHT UNTO A MAN, BUT HE END THEREOF ARE THE WAYS OF DEATH."PROVERBS 14:12

..IT IS APPOINTED UNTO MEN ONCE TO DIE, BUT AFTER THIS HE JUDGMENT."HEBREWS 9:27

..A MAN'S LIFE CONSISTETH NOT IN THE ABUNDANCE OF THE HINGS WHICH HE POSSESSETH."LUKE 12:15

OR WHAT SHALL IT PROFIT A MAN, IF HE SHALL GAIN THE HOLE WORLD, AND LOSE HIS OWN SOUL?" MARK 8:36

OR THE WAGES OF SIN IS DEATH: BUT THE GIFT OF GOD IS TERNAL LIFE THROUGH JESUS CHRIST OUR LORD." ROMANS 23

GOD HAS GIVEN TO US ETERNAL LIFE, AND THIS LIFE IS IN HIS ON." 1 JOHN 5:11

HESE ARE WRITTEN THAT YE MIGHT BELIEVE THAT JESUS IS HE CHRIST, THE SON OF GOD AND THAT BELIEVING YE IGHT HAVE LIFE THROUGH HIS NAME." JOHN 20:31

ND THIS IS LIFE ETERNAL, THAT THEY MIGHT KNOW THEE HE ONLY TRUE GOD, AND JESUS CHRIST, WHOM THOU HAST NT." JOHN 17:3

E THAT BELIEVETH ON THE SON, HATH EVERLASTING LIFE: ND HE THAT BELIEVETH NOT THE SON SHALL NOT SEE LIFE: UT THE WRATH OF GOD ABIDETH ON HIM." JOHN 3:36

OME NOW, AND LET US REASON TOGETHER, SAITH THE RD: THOUGH YOUR SINS BE AS SCARLET, THEY SHALL BE AS

WHITE AS SNOW; THOUGH THEY BE RED LIKE CRIMSON, THE
SHALL BE AS WOOL." ISAIAH 1:18

COMMITTED

YOU GAVE ME A NEW START
WHEN YOU TOUCHED MY HEART
SO I REPENTED
AND BECAME COMMITTED

TO YOUR WILL YOUR WAY
FOREVER CLOSE I'LL STAY
WHATEVER IT TAKES TO DO
GIVING MY ALL TO YOU

I HAVE BEEN FORGIVEN
RESTORED AND FREED FROM SIN
BY YOUR BLOOD I'M REDEEMED
RENEWED NOW I AM CLEANSED

THE VESSEL THAT IS READY
TO BE USED FOR YOUR GLORY
ENLIGHTENED BY THE HOLY SPIRIT
EMPOWERED AS I SUBMIT

FAITHFUL OR FALSE WITNESS

"A FAITHFUL WITNESS WILL NOT LIE: BUT A FALSE WITNESS WILL UTTER LIES." PROVERBS 14:5

"A TRUE WITNESS DELIVERETH SOULS: BUT A DECEITFUL WITNESS SPEAKETH LIES." PROVERBS 14:25

O GENERATION OF VIPERS, HOW CAN YE, BEING EVIL, SPEAK GOOD THINGS? FOR OUT OF THE ABUNDANCE OF THE HEART THE MOUTH SPEAKETH." MATTHEW 12:34

"A GOOD MAN OUT OF THE GOOD TREASURE OF THE HEART BRINGETH FORTH GOOD THINGS: AND AN EVIL MAN OUT OF THE EVIL TREASURE BRINGETH FORTH EVIL THINGS." MATTHEW 12:35

"BUT I SAY UNTO YOU, THAT EVERY IDLE WORD THAT MEN SHALL SPEAK, THEY SHALL GIVE ACCOUNT THEREOF IN THE DAY OF JUDGMENT." MATTHEW 12:36

OR BY THY WORDS THOU SHALT BE JUSTIFIED, AND BY THY
ORDS THOU SHALT BE CONDEMNED." MATTHEW 12:37

HE LIGHT OF THE BODY IS THE EYE: THEREFORE WHEN
HINE EYE IS SINGLE, THY WHOLE BODY ALSO IS FULL OF
IGHT; BUT WHEN THINE EYE IS EVIL, THY BODY ALSO IS FULL
F DARKNESS." LUKE 11:34

AKE HEED THEREFORE THAT THE LIGHT WHICH IS HID IN
HEE BE NOT DARKNESS." LUKE 11:35

OR EVERYONE THAT DOETH EVIL HATETH THE LIGHT,
EITHER COMETH TO THE LIGHT, BECAUSE THEIR DEEDS
ERE EVIL." JOHN 3:20

IE THAT COMMITTETH SIN IS OF THE DEVIL; FOR THE DEVIL
NNETH FROM THE BEGINNING. FOR THIS PURPOSE, THE SON
F GOD WAS MANIFESTED, THAT HE MIGHT DESTROY THE
ORKS OF THE DEVIL." 1 JOHN 3:8

WHOSOEVER IS BORN OF GOD DOTH NOT COMMIT SIN; FOR
IS SEED REMAINETH IN HIM: AND HE CANNOT SIN, BECAUSE
E IS BORN OF GOD." 1 JOHN 3:9

N THIS THE CHILDREN OF GOD ARE MANIFEST, AND THE
HILDREN OF THE DEVIL: WHOSOEVER DOETH NOT RIGHT-
OUSNESS IS NOT OF GOD, NEITHER HE THAT LOVETH NOT HIS
ROTHER." 1 JOHN 3:10

UT HE THAT DOETH TRUTH COMETH TO THE LIGHT, THAT
S DEEDS MAY BE MADE MANIFEST, THAT THEY ARE
ROUGHT IN GOD." JOHN 3:21

. THY WORD IS TRUTH." JOHN 17:17B

"...BLESSED ARE THEY THAT HEAR THE WORD OF GOD, AN̄
KEEP IT." LUKE 11:28

WHAT IF I WAS:

WORKING
HELPING
AVAILABLE
TEACHING

INTERCEDING
FORGIVING

WHAT IF I WAS:

WAVERING

HATING

ANGRY

TATTLING

IDLE

FAKE

ALSE

AKE

ND

ACKING

UFFICIENT

VIDENCE

RUTH

HE

EAL

NDENIABLE

ESTIMONY

OU HAVE A CHOICE TO BELIEVE WHAT IS FALSE OR THE RUTH!

HEAVEN

<u>**HELL**</u>

SALVATION

HE IS WAITING PATIENTLY
TO GIVE YOU LIFE ETERNALLY
BUT YOU MUST FIRST BELIEVE
IN ORDER TO RECEIVE

HE LOVES AND RESTORES
BUT THE CHOICE IS YOURS
DON'T MAKE THE MISTAKE
OF WAITING TOO LATE

POOR OR WEALTHY
SICK OR HEALTHY
BIG OR SMALL
SHORT OR TALL

WE ALL NEED HIM
WOMEN CHILDREN AND MEN
THE STRONG AND WEAK
JESUS IS WHOM WE MUST SEEK

BESIDES HIM THERE IS NONE
HE IS THE ONLY ONE
COME AND DON'T DELAY
GIVE YOUR LIFE TO CHRIST TODAY

I ONCE WAS THERE

I ONCE WAS THERE IN SIN
TORMENTED IN MY MIND
SPIRITUALLY DEAD WITHIN
NO PEACE I COULD FIND

UNTIL I ACCEPTED JESUS CHRIST
AS MY LORD AND SAVIOR
FOR ME HE SACRIFICED
HIS LIFE MY SINS HE BORED

THEN I WAS SET FREE
WITH LOVE JOY AND PEACE
HIS GOODNESS AND MERCY
NEVER EVER CEASE

HIS SPIRIT IS IN ME
I REPRESENT HIM
THE LOVE OF CHRIST INTERNALLY
EVERLASTING LIFE WITH HIM

SO YOU ASK IF I REALLY CARE
YES I DO I TRULY DO
BECAUSE I ONCE WAS THERE
THAT'S WHY I CARE ABOUT YOU

THERE WAS A VOID

THERE WAS A VOID
THAT I COULD NOT FILL
TRIED THINGS OF THIS WORLD
BUT I WAS EMPTY STILL

JESUS BLOOD CLEANSED
AND REMOVED MY SINS
HIS LOVE FILLED ME
AND HIS SPIRIT IS WITHIN

SILVER AND GOLD
FOR I HAVE NONE
BUT MORE VALUABLE
JESUS GOD'S SON

YES HE IS

THE ANSWER

AND TO YOU

I'D LIKE TO OFFER

GOD CAN RESTORE

IN THE PAST MY FEELINGS
I TRIED TO CONCEAL
MISERABLE AS I WAS
NEVER WANTING TO REVEAL

WHAT WAS I TRYING TO PROVE
I REALLY DON'T KNOW
BUT ONE THING IS CERTAIN
JESUS IS THE ONE TO FOLLOW

WITH HIM YOU WON'T GO WRONG
HE WILL NEVER LEAD YOU ASTRAY
HE CAME AS A SACRIFICIAL LAMB
A REDEEMER I WOULD SAY

BEING MADE FREE FROM SIN
WE BECAME SERVANTS OF RIGHTEOUSNESS
ETERNAL LIFE THROUGH JESUS CHRIST
HIS NAME I WILL FOREVER BLESS

THROUGH HIM I WAS REBORN
NOT MISERABLE ANYMORE
BUT A NEW LIFE OF PEACE AND JOY
YES GOD CAN RESTORE

LORD I AM YOURS

FAITHFULLY
LORD I AM YOURS
COMPLETELY

LORD I THANK YOU
I'M GRATEFUL
LORD I BLESS YOU
FOR YOU ARE FAITHFUL

THANK YOU

**THANK YOU LORD FOR ALLOWING ME
TO BEHOLD NATURE'S BEAUTY
ANOTHER DAY TO LIVE AND SEE
ANOTHER CHANCE AND OPPORTUNITY**

AS I SEEK YOU AND STRIVE TO BE
MORE AND MORE LIKE THEE
THE HOLY SPIRIT WITHIN GUIDING
TO DO AND SAY WHAT IS PLEASING

THANK YOU LORD FOR WISDOM
KNOWLEDGE I WELCOME
UNDERSTANDING OF YOUR KINGDOM
AS GIVEN TO KING SOLOMON

YOUR ENDING

YOUR ENDING
NOT YOUR BEGINNING
IS PREPARED FOR YOU
SO CONTINUE

FAMILY FRIENDS AND SOME
DISAPPOINTMENTS MAY COME
GOING THROUGH THE VALLEY
WILL HELP REACH YOUR DESTINY

EXPECT IT
ACCEPT IT
BUT BE STRONG
AND HOLD ON

FOCUS YOUR EYES
ON THE PRIZE
OF THE HIGHEST CALLING
TOWARD THE MARK KEEP PRESSING

DON'T LOOK BACK
IT'S A FACT
YOU CAN'T REACH YOUR REWARD
IF YOU DON'T GO FORWARD

A TIME IN MY LIFE

THERE WAS A TIME IN MY LIFE
WHEN I THOUGHT I HAD IT ALL
BUT AS I CLIMBED THE LADDER
I STARTED TO FALL

THERE WAS A TIME IN MY LIFE
THAT I FELT SO SECURE
THOUGHT I DIDN'T NEED ANYONE
IN MY PRESENT OR FUTURE

THERE WAS A TIME IN MY LIFE
I DIDN'T KNOW I WAS BLESSED
UNTIL I WAS AT THE POINT
OF FEELING HOPELESS

THEN CAME A TIME IN MY LIFE
SALVATION I RECEIVED
JESUS CHRIST AS MY LORD AND SAVIOR
WHEN I BELIEVED

A TIME IN MY LIFE
I REALIZED MY PURPOSE THAT DAY
TO DO THE WILL OF GOD
TRUST HIM PRAY AND OBEY

NOW I'M AT A TIME
WHERE I AM CONFIDENT
A TIME IN MY LIFE
WHERE I AM CONTENT

I AM SO GRATEFUL
JESUS HAS SET ME FREE
WITH HIM I AM VICTORIOUS
AND GIVE HIM HONOR AND GLORY

TRANSFORMATION

MADE WRONG CHOICES IN THE PAST
RELATIONSHIPS THAT DIDN'T LAST
BLINDED BY SIN I WENT ASTRAY
SEEKED GOD AND HE SHOWED ME THE WAY

THEN A TRANSFORMATION TOOK PLACE
IT IS REVEALED ALL OVER MY FACE
THERE IS LOVE IN MY HEART
AND NOW I'VE BEEN GIVEN A FRESH START

NO LONGER BLIND
PEACE IN MY MIND
LOVE UNCONDITIONAL
JOY UNSPEAKABLE

JESUS IS THE ONLY WAY

**JESUS CHRIST IS THE ONLY
WAY TO OUR HEAVENLY
FATHER AND GOD OF HUMANITY
CAME TO SET THE CAPTIVES FREE**

HONOR AND GLORY
IS DUE TO THEE
I PRAISE GOD CONTINUALLY
FOR MY VICTORY

THROUGH JESUS WHO SAVED ME
AND DELIVERED ME
FROM BURNING ETERNALLY
A CONDEMNED DESTINY

LORD AND SAVIOR IS HE
PRAISE I GIVE THEE
NO LONGER BOUND I'M FREE
ACCORDING TO JOHN CHAPTER THREE

**HAVE YOU ACCEPTED THE GIFT (JESUS)
I SENT YOU
OVER 2000 YEARS AGO?
LOVE,
GOD**

NOTES

Made in the USA
Columbia, SC
27 September 2023

23358842R00065